D0324391

PET OWNER'S GUIDE TO THE
OLD ENGLISH SHEEPDOG

Ruth Wilkinson

RINGPRESS

ABOUT THE AUTHOR

Pockethall is the name of a field in Horwich belonging to Ruth Wilkinson's family and it is also the affix for her world-famous Old English Sheepdogs. Her mother showed and bred Sheepdogs when she was a young girl and that started Ruth's lifelong passion for this lovely breed. The first time Ruth encountered an Old English Sheepdog was when she was about five years old. In the middle of the hearth she saw what she thought was a fluffy black and white ball. When she went to investigate it, she realized that it was a small puppy. From then on, Bobtails have been part of her life.

Ruth and her husband, Ray, bought their first Old English Sheepdog in 1969. He was Roncot Blue Cloud, known as Blue. Friends talked them into showing him and, on his first appearance in the ring, in a Minor Puppy Class, he was placed fourth out of a class of thirty-six.

Their first Champion was Ch. Cornelia of Trimtora, called Lyn, who produced Ch. Pockethall New Shoes, Ch. Pockethall Blue Cloud, Ch. Pockethall Silver Shoes and Ch. Pockethall Shoe Shine of Southview. These dogs went on to produce star progeny.

Ruth is a respected international show judge, invited by the Kennel Club to judge and award CCs at Crufts in 2001. Her dogs have been exported around the world and shown successfully in many countries. Through her involvement with Old English Sheepdogs, she and Ray have made friends both at home and internationally.

ACKNOWLEDGEMENTS

The publisher would like to thank the following for their help with photography: Janet Swannell (Breedonhill), Carolyne Haynes (Achardia), Pauline Barnes (Macopa), Margaret Hulbert (Targamar), and Chris and Eve Jones (Wenalt).

Designed by: Rob Benson

Published by Ringpress Books Limited,
PO Box 8, Lydney, Gloucestershire,
GL15 4YN, United Kingdom.

First published 2002
©2002 Ringpress Books Limited. All rights reserved

ISBN 1 86054 104 6

Printed and bound in Hong Kong through Printworks International Ltd.

CONTENTS

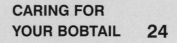

1 Introducing The Old English Sheepdog

The Old English Sheepdog is a wonderful, immediately recognisable dog, with a distinctive coat and a great fall of hair over his eyes.

As we shall see, different breed historians have offered various theories about how these characteristics developed. What we do know is that the Bobtail, which is the affectionate name for these dogs, is a very special animal. In more formal circles, the name is abbreviated to OES.

Old English Sheepdogs were originally used for herding and guarding livestock.

The Bearded Collie is smaller, but bears a strong similarity to the Bobtail.

ORIGINS

There is speculation that the Old English Sheepdog developed from the Himalayan herding dog, which was larger than the Bobtail, but there are similarities. The Russian Sheepdog is also said to be an ancestor. This, again, is a larger breed than the Bobtail, but the type and colour are very similar. Another close relation, but smaller in type, is the Bearded Collie.

In the beginning, matings of various sheepdogs were not planned and breeders did not keep records, but there is evidence, through artefacts, of what the Bobtail looked like then.

The earliest probable depiction of an Old English Sheepdog is in a painting by Gainsborough, dated 1771, showing the Duke of Buccleuch with his arms around an Old English type of dog.

WORKING DOGS

Bobtails were used to herd cattle and drive sheep to market. It was very common, decades ago, to see livestock being driven to market by working dogs, dogs who had docked tails. Owners of dogs with tails paid a tax: working dogs were exempt. The breed is still customarily docked in the UK and the US.

It is also believed that the Bobtail was a guard dog, looking after the shepherd and his flock at night.

EVOLUTION

The Old English Sheepdog evolved naturally, performing certain tasks for man, and adapting to different climates. He originated, quite simply, from stock which served man, helped guard livestock and protected the farms and homes of the herdsmen.

The Bobtail today still waits for his master's commands. These are very intelligent dogs and you will find that most Bobtails, when out walking with you in the park, will herd the family.

COAT

One of the great characteristics

The long, thick coat is an outstanding characteristic of the breed – but your dog will only look like this after a lengthy bathing and grooming session.

Sometimes more human than dog, the OES loves to join in with family activities.

of the Bobtail is his coat. It grows long and thick, with a dense undercoat. Care and attention must be started at an early age – in fact as soon as your puppy is settled in his new home and within the first day or so.

The coat markings do not really matter unless you want to show, and I always say that it is what is underneath the coat that is important. However, if you are thinking that you may, at a later date, want to show your Bobtail, it is not advisable to purchase a puppy that has white markings in the grey or darker part of the body. This is known as a flash and should not be encouraged.

A Bobtail has a double coat, with long guard hairs and a thick undercoat, which keeps him dry in wet weather, enables him to withstand very icy weather, and yet helps to keep him cool in the summer.

CHARACTER

An Old English Sheepdog makes a lovely family pet. But, on the other hand, he thinks he is human and not a dog!

These dogs make good guards for your home, mainly because of their very deep bark that soon puts people off. However, be warned, they also soon make a friend. They just love people. One way they keep guard is that, when one of the family has gone out, they listen to all the different sounds and only relax when that family member returns home.

The OES is full of character and is a very strong animal when fully grown. It is very important to start training as soon as you take your puppy to his new home. If taught with care, he will be only too delighted to please.

BOBTAILS AND CHILDREN

The Old English Sheepdog is a brilliant family dog, who adores children. He can be a little boisterous, especially when young,

Little and large: This Bobtail and Lhasa Apso have learned to live in harmony.

though, so teach your puppy very early on to respect all members of the family.

If he gets too rowdy, he must be calmed down. Sternly, tell him to "Sit". If he jumps up at children (or anyone else), tell him "Off", and gently push him down. Then ignore him. All dogs hate being ignored, and he'll soon learn that jumping up is no fun at all.

To prevent food-bowl guarding, involve your children when feeding your puppy.

Ask them to give the puppy his bowl, to take it away when he is half-way through his meal, and then to give it back to him again. Your puppy will grow up thinking it is perfectly right that the family can touch or take away his bowl,

and this should prevent possessive behaviour later in life.

OTHER ANIMALS

The Bobtail will get on well with other pets, such as cats and other dogs. I do think it is wise, though, if you have other dogs, to bring in a puppy, who will fit in far better than an older dog. Older dogs are set in their own ways and can sometimes be jealous. I have known cases where two older dogs never became friends and this can be a great problem for all the family. Older dogs, surprisingly enough, will put up with a lot from a young animal, and puppies learn to take notice of an older dog. They will be just fine together.

2 Choosing An Old English Sheepdog

Y ou really need to think carefully before buying an OES. Ask yourself, and your family, whether this is the type of dog you all want. The Bobtail is a lovely animal, which will fit into any family and, with the love and attention you give him, will be a very faithful pet and friend in return. The Bobtail just loves to be with you all the time, wherever you might be in your home. You will find that these dogs do not like to be left alone, even if you have only gone to the bathroom.

The Bobtail now is not quite so popular as he was in the 1970s and 80s, which is not a bad thing because undue popularity can ruin a breed. However, despite this, there are quite a number of Bobtails still having to be rescued, for many different reasons. Therefore, it is very important, if you decide you really want an Old English Sheepdog, that you are absolutely sure you will be able to give the dog a home for life. The OES is a very lively animal and needs plenty of time and attention.

Bobtail puppies are irresistible, but think long and hard before taking the plunge into ownership.

At a dog show you will be able to see many different Bobtails, and, after showing is completed, you can talk to the exhibitors who will have considerable knowledge of the breed.

MALE OR FEMALE?

If you are considering purchasing your first OES then, in my opinion, a dog puppy would be best. People think a bitch may be better, but I find dogs really rely on you so much more than a bitch. Bitches are very independent and most of them have seasons every six months – though this can vary, and a particular bitch may come into season every four months.

Dogs, of course, do not have seasons, so it is one less problem to worry about. However, dogs can have a habit of mounting. Never allow your young dog to try to mount you, or any other human being. To stop this behaviour, tell him "No", as a very firm instruction, but do not shout.

14

If he continues, tell him to sit or lie down. You must, however, try not to make an issue of it, because, if he is a show-quality animal, you may want to use him for stud when he is older. Another ploy is to walk away from your dog if he shows any inclination to mount you.

NEUTERING

If you are new to the breed, and do not intend to show or breed from your dog, then neutering is the best option. It can prevent many health problems, such as pyometra (page 79) or mammary tumours in the bitch, or prostate disorders in the dog.

Neutering your bitch will stop her seasons, and will prevent unwanted pregnancies. Neutering a dog will stop him straying off after bitches, and, in most cases, mounting.

Neutering can make a dog or bitch predisposed to weight gain, so monitor your Bobtail closely to ensure the pounds do not start piling on. A slight reduction in his daily food allowance should be all that is necessary.

Your vet will discuss the advantages and disadvantages of neutering with you, explaining the ideal time to perform the operation, and answering any questions you may have.

If you meet a few adult Bobtails together, you will get an impression of what it is like living with large, hairy dogs!

DOCKING

Most newborn Old English Sheepdog puppies (from 12 to 48 hours old) have their tails docked by a vet. If you would like a puppy with a tail, you must let the breeder know before the litter is born. Many breeders refuse to sell undocked pups.

REPUTABLE BREEDERS

When you and your family have really made up your minds, are sure that you do want an OES, and have decided on the sex you prefer, and whether you would like a docked or undocked puppy, then it is time to contact a reputable breeder.

Your national kennel club will be able to provide you with details of your nearest OES Breed Club Secretary, who will be able to put you in touch with breeders who may have puppies. Breeders will also be glad to keep you in mind for any future litter they are planning.

Most breeders will be more than happy to talk to you about the Bobtail, especially if you are not sure what you are letting yourself in for and wish to ask a number of questions.

The breeder will help you to assess the puppies in terms of both temperament and conformation.

The best way to make up your mind about buying an OES is by seeing three or more dogs come bounding into the lounge of the house where they live, barking with excitement. This either makes buyers more determined, or completely turns them off. You may think that you would not be able to cope with such a large dog when it is full-grown. You will also be able to see the amount of coat an adult dog will have.

Another way of discovering where to obtain your puppy is by going to a dog show. Throughout the world, there are so many publications devoted to canine matters that you will be able to find out, through them, the schedules for shows in your area. At these shows, you will be able to meet and speak to different breeders and discover the dogs that you particularly like.

It is important to see the puppies' mother as she will give some indication of how the puppies will turn out.

ASSESSING A LITTER

You must purchase a well-reared puppy, whether you only want a pet or whether you are thinking that, perhaps, you may decide to start showing. It is very important to see the dam of the pups. More often than not, the sire will live in a different part of the country at another kennel, so it is unlikely

that you will be able to see him. However, there might be a photograph available.

A well-reared puppy should stand sturdily, with very strong legs and a nice straight front. The hocks should be short and, when viewed from the rear, be well apart and straight. When you move round the puppy, he should be bold and not cowering or frightened.

When you are choosing a puppy, take care to look for different reactions in the litter. If you see that a puppy is asleep and not taking any notice of anything that is happening round him, this could be a sign that the puppy is deaf. Do not be frightened to make any noises, clapping your hands, or shouting, anything to catch the attention of the puppy which is sleeping. Puppies that are deaf will not respond.

They will react to being touched if you tickle any part of their body, or even if one of the littermates walks over them. This will make such a puppy take notice and follow what his littermates are doing.

BUYING THE BEST

I always say you might as well have the best, whether you are buying a pet or a possible show puppy. A puppy you want to show should catch your eye and attention. Watch how the puppies move and how they carry themselves.

You could buy a potential show puppy from a breeder, but you must remember the words 'show potential'. That potential may not be realised, and only time will tell. When you take your puppy home you will have a lot of work to do to enable him to become a dog that you can take into the ring and show. This is not easy and needs a lot of time and effort.

THE MOUTH

An Old English Sheepdog should have a strong jaw with the bite being well over; this means that,

Watch the puppies playing together so you can get an idea of individual characters.

If you are planning to show your Bobtail, points of conformation must be evaluated.

THE SKULL

Look for a broad skull that seems square, with the eyes well apart. The puppy should also have small, low-set ears, flat to the side of the head, and a nice, arched neck. If you run your hand over the puppy from the shoulders, along the backbone over to the loin, you should be able to feel a gentle rise from the shoulder to the rump. The rib cage should be nicely covered. If the puppy is very strong and stocky-looking at the rib cage, this should seem very deep.

at six or seven weeks old, the top teeth should be over the bottom teeth; not level and most certainly not undershot or overshot. If you notice a puppy with his tongue always hanging between the teeth when the mouth is closed, this is an indication that the mouth will not be good when fully grown. The mouth will more than likely be a wry mouth. This means that, when the OES has changed from baby teeth to adult teeth, the mouth will not close properly. This is classed as a big problem, especially if you want to breed from the dog later on. That wry mouth will be passed on to the progeny.

PIGMENTATION

The eyes should be a dark grey or deep midnight blue, with signs of pigmentation on the eyelids. The darker the eye colour at an early age, the better. When they change

The skull should be broad and the eyes set well apart.

Coat markings do not matter at this age, but avoid a coat that is flashed.

to brown they will be dark. You may find that some puppies are wall-eyed. This means that the puppy will have one brown and one blue eye, or even have two blue eyes. A puppy with plenty of pigmentation will have his nose filled in very early, in the first weeks of his life. If a puppy has no pigment and just pink eyelids, this is not a good sign and this variation is given the name 'piggy eyes'. Pigment is very important, especially if you intend to breed from your Bobtail.

COAT MARKING
Markings do not really matter, although I do not recommend a puppy that is flashed, which means that there are white markings in the dark part of the puppy's body. If you are thinking of showing your puppy, a white front and neck look good, but are not the most important parts. It is what is underneath the coat that counts. The Old English Sheepdog, when being shown, is what is known as a 'hands-on' breed, which means that the judge will handle the dog in order to feel what lies underneath the outer covering.

BREED STANDARD SUMMARY
The Old English Sheepdog is a strong, square-looking dog with great symmetry and is profusely coated all over. This is a thick-set, muscular, able-bodied dog with a

The square, symmetrical build of an Old English Sheepdog.

most intelligent expression. The dog's natural outline should not be artificially changed by scissoring or clipping.

The height of dogs should be 22 inches (56 cms) and upwards and bitches slightly smaller. Type and symmetry are of greatest importance, and on no account to be sacrificed to size alone.

The dogs have great stamina and their bodies look pear-shaped when viewed from above. Their gait has a typical roll when ambling or walking. Their bark has a distinctive tonal quality.

These are biddable dogs of even disposition. They are bold, faithful and trustworthy, with no suggestion of nervousness or unprovoked aggression.

FOREQUARTERS

In proportion to the size of the body, the skull is capacious and rather square. The muzzle is strong, square and truncated, measuring approximately half of the total head length. The nose is large and black with wide nostrils. The eyes are set well apart. Light eyes are undesirable. Pigmentation on the rim is preferred. The ears are small and carried flat to the side of the head.

The teeth are strong, large, and evenly placed. The jaws are strong with a perfect, regular and complete scissor bite, which means the upper teeth closely overlap the lower teeth and are set square to the jaws.

The neck is fairly long and

When viewed from the rear, the Bobtail has a bear-like roll.

Effortless extension is seen when the dog is trotting.

strong and arched gracefully. The forelegs are perfectly straight, with plenty of bone. The elbows fit close to brisket. The shoulders should be well laid back, being narrower at the point of withers than at the point of shoulder.

HINDQUARTERS
The loin is very sturdy, broad and gently arched, the quarters are well covered, round and muscular, the second thigh is long and well developed, the stifle well turned, and the hocks set low. From the rear, hocks should be quite straight, with the feet turning neither in nor out.

The feet should be small, round and tight, with the toes well arched, and the pads thick and hard. Dewclaws should be removed and the tail is customarily completely docked.

MOVEMENT
When walking, the dog has a bear-like roll when seen from the rear. When trotting, the dog shows effortless extension and a strong

The head and skull are well covered with hair.

driving rear action, with legs moving straight along the line of travel and very elastic at the gallop. At slow speeds, some dogs may tend to pace. When moving, the head carriage may adopt a naturally lower position.

COAT

The coat is profuse and of a good harsh texture, not straight, but shaggy and free from curl. There is an undercoat of waterproof pile. The head and skull are well covered with hair, the ears are moderately coated, the neck is well coated, the forelegs are well coated all round. The hindquarters are more heavily coated than the rest of the body.

The dog's coat colour can be any shade of grey, grizzle or blue. The body and hindquarters are of solid colour with or without white socks. White patches in the solid area are to be discouraged. The head, neck, forequarters and underbelly should be white, with or without markings. Any shade of brown is undesirable.

3 *Caring For Your Bobtail*

When he is eight weeks old, it is time to bring your new puppy home. It is a good idea to introduce him to a routine immediately; this will help both him and everyone in the family.

PREPARATIONS

Before you bring your puppy home, there are a few things you need to sort out. Decide where your puppy is going to sleep, eat and exercise. You may want him only to go into certain rooms, mainly until you know whether you can trust him about accidents.

When the family have decided where the puppy will be allowed to go, you must make sure that your garden is completely safe and secure, and that all holes, if any, are sealed and any gates can be locked so that no one is able to leave a gate open by mistake. Always remember the golden rule, *safety first*.

Bobtail puppies are great explorers, so it is important to check that both your house and garden are safe and secure.

GARDEN

If you have a pond in the garden, you must always keep it covered over with a net, or drain the water away, or fence it in. Otherwise you can be absolutely certain that the puppy will end up in the pond.

You will have to keep any poisonous shrubs out of reach, but the best thing is to remove them from the areas where your puppy will go. Most evergreens are a danger to animals.

HOME

Make sure all electrical and telephone wires are out of reach. These are all dangerous for your puppy. An accident can happen very quickly.

You will find that the puppy will like your clothing, especially clothes which have been worn. He will raid your linen basket and will chew buttons off cardigans or shirts and blouses. Some of the best-liked things are shoes and slippers. Make sure you keep the linen basket, and anything you treasure, out of harm's way.

Always make sure your puppy has something to play with. Very good toys to buy are those that you can leave with the puppy when you are going out. They can be filled with goodies, which you

know your puppy loves. It takes time for your puppy to empty them. He will then be tired and go to sleep for an hour or so.

PUPPY'S OWN PLACE

It is very important that you train your puppy to have his own place, which you can call your puppy's bed. The kitchen or utility room are the best places for this. Make a bed by placing a nice fleecy blanket on the floor. I think just making a bed on the floor is right for an OES, because you will find, when they are fully grown, that is where they prefer to sleep. Fleecy blankets are the best. You are able to keep the blankets clean because they are easily washed in the washing machine and soon dry. More often than not they are almost dry when you take them from the washer, if spun on a high speed.

Alternatively, you can buy thick, fleecy, veterinary bedding. This material will keep your puppy clean and dry and, if he has an accident, the urine just goes through the bedding. However, you will need to change the bedding often. The best thing is to have about three of these blankets so that you can keep changing them regularly.

With a careful introduction, most puppies learn to accept a crate.

Never leave your puppy confined in his crate for long periods.

You can buy a folding cage, which is very portable, but you should not use the cage all of the time. Your young puppy will get to like the cage, but also needs the freedom to walk and play when he wants to do so. Short periods only are acceptable in a cage and it can be a peaceful place of refuge in which a puppy can rest securely, when you are not able to supervise him (for example, at night).

JOURNEY HOME

When you collect your puppy, it is a good idea for two people to go along. You will need some newspapers, a blanket, and some paper kitchen towels which are handy for cleaning up any accidents which may occur. Have a bowl and a container filled with water so that your puppy can have a drink on the way home. Remember also to ask the breeder for some food, the same food that your puppy has been eating, so that there is less chance of him having an upset stomach during his first few days with you. At this stage, do not worry if he will not take a drink; just give him time to settle and get used to his new surroundings.

Bringing a puppy home by car for the first time and with strange people, can be very traumatic. To help the puppy settle, the best idea is to let him sit with you on the back seat of the car or even on your knee, not rattling around alone. This should help him to settle down and not be too frightened.

On no occasion let your puppy on to the ground when you are travelling home, even if your journey is a long one, as he will not have had all his puppy vaccinations and may pick up a dangerous disease. When you have arrived home, you then can allow him to go on the ground, outside, in the place you have already prepared for him.

Sometimes when you bring a new puppy home, he may have an upset stomach. This is why it is advisable to bring home with you some of the same diet that your puppy has been eating while being weaned from the dam. If he does have an upset stomach, do not rush off to the vet; it should clear up the following day. If you are not happy and the sickness persists, then is the time to contact the vet.

ARRIVING HOME

When you arrive home, first take

Give your puppy a chance to explore his new surroundings.

your puppy to the place in which you wish him to relieve himself (see below). Then let him meet the family and investigate his new home.

The puppy's food should be situated in the place where you are going to let him always eat his food. His bed should be located somewhere quiet, where he can rest undisturbed. Puppies need lots of sleep, and, with all the excitement of moving home, your new arrival will probably need to rest after he has finished all his investigating.

HOUSE-TRAINING

Take your puppy outside to the place you want him to relieve himself, ask him to spend a penny, or do his toilet, or whatever. The point is that you should use a particular word which he will soon realise means that you want him to do his duty. The sooner you start training, the better.

Always let a puppy out to relieve himself whenever you have given him a meal or a drink. If you hear him giving little cries and wandering around, possibly looking for the door, then this a good indication that he needs to go out. If your puppy does have an accident in the house, never scold him. It was probably your fault that it happened, because you had not been paying enough attention to his signals, and had not taken him outside enough. Just take him outside and be gentle and patient with him.

EARLY TRAINING

When training, always keep the same words or phrases matched to a particular action, so that soon your puppy will associate the word with the deed. You can start

straight away, by cleaning your puppy's feet and wiping his mouth before you go inside. Then, when your puppy is fully grown, you will find he will always wait until you have wiped his feet and dried his beard. This will help you to keep both your dog and your house clean.

BEDTIME

You will find that, when you leave your puppy at bedtime for the first few nights, he may cry and bark. You must try to block the noise out, otherwise you will be making trouble for yourself. Your puppy will soon get used to the idea of bedtime, especially when you put the lights out.

Changing homes is a traumatic business, and most puppies will be unsettled for the first few days.

You will find that your puppy may cry when left on his own. Remember that he has been used to a lot of noise and company. If you do not have any other family or pets, he may feel quite lonely. You will have to keep him company or, maybe, you can leave a radio on, so that he will not feel too isolated.

Early in the morning, if you hear your puppy crying, you must go and attend to him, because he may want to relieve himself. If you ignore the cries, you will find it much harder to house-train him. You must always listen to your puppy. He may go to the door and start to cry. He is telling you that he needs to go out in order to relieve himself in the proper place.

FEEDING

When puppies are going to a new home, the breeder should give you a diet sheet, and its advice can last throughout your dog's life, or until you are confident about how to look after the dog yourself.

Give your puppy any of the following meals for breakfast: milk, rice pudding, porridge or cereal. Puppies like evaporated milk that you can mix with cool, boiled water and with the rice

To begin with, feed the diet that the puppy's breeder has recommended.

pudding or any cereal. When puppies are very young, they like to eat sweeter food. Dried milk is the best to use for puppies. You will find they will drink about two pints per day of this preparation and even more when they are starting to grow.

At midday, feed your puppy with a meat meal: mix together the meat and puppy-meal, you can also mix dried kelp and a few drops of cod liver oil. Kelp can be given in tablet form. You must follow the instructions given on the label for the correct dosage. You can feed all different kinds of meat to your puppy such as raw minced (finely-chopped) meat, chicken, fish and tinned dog food. There are many different varieties.

If you choose to use tinned, or canned, food, then you must start from the very beginning, once your puppy has settled in and has no tummy upsets, to feed him with these food varieties. I prefer to feed puppies with natural foods, rather than the easy way with all-in-one dried food.

Make sure that you cook chicken and fish completely, removing all the bones, which can be very dangerous and make your dog extremely sick. Good-quality meat or minced (finely-chopped) meat can be given raw, but must always be fresh.

BROWN BREAD MIXER

Brown bread is one of the best mixers you can use with any kind of meat, fish and chicken, because it will keep the dog's motions nice and firm. The OES is prone to loose motions. Brown bread will certainly help in this department.

FEEDING BOWLS

Stainless steel bowls are the best. They are easy to keep clean and you can even put them in the dishwasher. They will not scratch, as plastic will, so bacteria will not lodge in any crevices. In the first months, your puppy will require two small stainless steel dishes, but you will find that you require two large bowls very soon. If you use plastic bowls, you will find that your puppy will chew the edges, they will become very rough and you will not be able to keep them nice and clean.

PUPPY DRINKS

Always give milk to your puppy first thing in the morning and last thing at night, when you are putting him to bed. You will find he will usually sleep after having a drink of milk. I never let any of my puppies drink water until they are older. I feel that milk is better. If you are feeding dried milk, you have to mix the powder with water in any case. I use dried milk powder because ordinary cow's milk will give some dogs diarrhoea.

Whenever you make your milk, always make sure you use boiled water. It is a good idea, when you have used the water in the kettle, to refill it and boil another kettleful. In this way, you will always have some boiled water ready for use at any time.

When your puppy is fully grown, you must make sure that fresh water is always available. The only time my dogs do not have access to water is when I collect all the water dishes up and wash them in very hot water.

I always give my Old English Sheepdogs fresh water first thing in the morning; I find that they do not drink a great deal during the day but always like a good drink of water before they go to bed at night.

FEEDING SCHEDULE

With a young puppy, always rotate between milk/cereal meals and meat meals. As stated previously, the last meal at night should always be a drink of milk. When your puppy is about four months old, you can always give him a large biscuit. He will soon catch on to the idea that when you leave him, you will give him

As your puppy grows, the number of meals can be gradually reduced until you are feeding just one meal a day. A raised bowl helps to keep the coat out of the food.

AGE	NO. OF MEALS
8 weeks	6 (2 meat meals, 4 milk meals)
12 weeks	5 (2 meat meals, 3 milk meals)
16 weeks	4 (2 meat meals, 2 milk meals)
20 weeks	3 (2 meat meals, 1 milk meal)
6 months	2 (2 meat meals)
1 year	1 (meat meal), though some people prefer to continue feeding two meals throughout the dog's life

a treat. This also helps to take your puppy's mind off your departure.

When you are going to give your puppy a treat, train him to sit at your command and tell him not to grab, but to take it nicely.

Never leave unwanted food on the floor. Always give your puppy enough time to eat his meal. Then, if he leaves any food, just pick up the bowl and throw away the food. You could keep it in a fridge for a short period of time, but be very careful, because food can soon go off and, if consumed, will then upset your puppy's stomach.

In the beginning, your puppy will be on about five or six meals a day. You will find that he will gradually cut down his meals himself, until he only requires one meal per day. This is the natural way for him to progress. You can, of course, give him milk for as long as you like. My dogs will always drink milk, even though they are adults.

The breeder will provide you with approximate quantities of how much you should be feeding. Quantities will vary according to the type of food you are using, so always read the manufacturer's instructions carefully.

Provide safe toys for your puppy to chew when he is teething.

TREATS

In pet stores you can buy toys that you are able to fill with treats. As I have said, these are a really good idea, enabling you to give your puppy a treat which involves a game, as well as helping him to pass the time while you are doing your own work. Remember to buy large toys rather than small ones which can be quite dangerous. I have known even large dogs to choke on a small ball.

The leather-type bones should not be given to your dog. The very large ones with big knots, when wet, can slip down the throat, get stuck and choke the dog.

Small balls can be just as dangerous, especially if your puppy jumps and catches the ball in his mouth. The ball can quite easily slip down the puppy's throat and, once again, get stuck. A large, hard, rubber ball is recommended and your puppy will have a great deal of fun playing with it.

Never encourage games of tug-of-war, which can be harmful to a dog's mouth and teeth.

SECOND TEETH

There is always a potential problem when your puppy is changing teeth. His mouth will be very sore. This can be very distressful. If your puppy is hurt at this time, at this early stage in his life, he will always remember it. If you go to training classes and you know that your puppy's mouth is very tender, just ask the trainer not to bother looking at it, because you know this will be counterproductive.

Make sure you are able to handle your puppy's mouth without hurting him. I advise you to keep handling and touching his mouth as often as possible, but being gentle, of course. This will help him and give him confidence when he is being handled by the vet or by a judge in the show ring.

Puppies usually start changing their teeth from about ten weeks onwards. Bitches usually start before dogs. Do not remove any baby teeth, unless they are very loose. In that case, just push outwards towards the outer gum or lip and you will find that the loose teeth will just move and fall out.

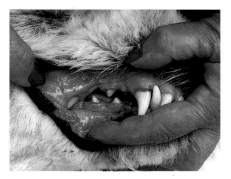

The adult teeth have now come through.

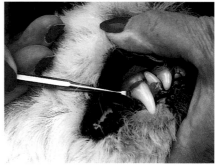

If tartar has accumulated, you will need to enlist the help of a vet or an experienced groomer to remove it.

EXERCISING YOUR BOBTAIL

Puppies get all the exercise they need by playing in the garden.

The adult Bobtail (below) is a lively, energetic dog, who will make good use of his outings.

Make sure that your puppy has something hard to chew, such as a big knuckle-bone. He will love this and it will help him keep his teeth clean. Remember to make sure that any bones you allow him to have are always fresh from the butcher.

CHEWS

Pet stores supply all kinds of different chewing things which are good for youngsters and for later in life. There are very hard plastic bones and other different kinds of shapes. I advise you to buy something large enough for your puppy to be able to use later in his life. Another good thing about hard, plastic, shaped bones is that you are able to clean them in the dishwasher.

When your puppy has acquired all his second teeth, you do need to check for any build-up of tartar or plaque. You can buy, from most pet stores, toothpaste in different flavours and a toothbrush that you are able to use to clean your dog's teeth each day or at least once or twice each week. The other way to keep your dog's teeth clean is by buying a special descaling instrument comparable to the one your own dentist uses. But be warned, you will have to be

very careful when using this sort of equipment.

EXERCISE

The Old English Sheepdog is quite a large breed, and can be prone to hip dysplasia (page 78), so particular care must be taken to ensure his bones and joints are given time to grow and strengthen before they are subjected to excess stress.

Jumping up, climbing the stairs, etc. must be prevented until he is 12-18 months old when his bones and joints will be stronger and he will have completed the majority of his growing. Until this time, exercise should be carefully controlled.

Until the puppy has had his vaccinations, playing in the garden will suffice. When he is first taken out for walks, keep them short. A five-minute walk to the park, some play, and then the short walk back home again will be more than enough. Gradually build up the length of exercise periods until he is 12-18 months old, when he can enjoy longer, more challenging walks.

When walking with an adult Bobtail, remember that he will walk at least five times more distance than you. Because of

The elderly Bobtail is a loving and affectionate companion and deserves special consideration.

his herding background, he is likely to run off to play, then return to his family, circle them to make sure everyone is present and correct, and then run off to investigate and play again. So 10-mile hikes twice a day are really not necessary – he will be getting more than enough exercise in two 20-minute walks.

VETERAN CARE

When looking after older Bobtails, each case is different. Most older dogs sleep more, and some may want less exercise. Because they are using less energy, they may not need as much food, so keep an eye on your dog to make sure he does not become overweight. Obesity in dogs is very dangerous, putting undue pressure on the heart and joints, so if you find it difficult to keep your dog's weight down (particularly a problem in neutered animals), ask your vet for advice. Many practices hold specialist weight loss clinics.

For some oldies, the problem is not overeating, but loss of appetite. Feeding three small meals a day is preferable, in such cases, to giving one large feed. You may have to experiment with different flavours to stimulate your Bobtail's appetite. Smelly foods, such as fish flavours, often do the trick.

If your older Bobtail finds it a nuisance to be groomed for hours on end, you might consider giving him a pet trim (see page 51) or having him clipped off.

EUTHANASIA

Putting a dog to sleep is always a difficult decision, but, sadly, it is one that all pet owners face at one time or another.

If your dog is sick, and is suffering, and all avenues of treatment have been explored to no avail, you should consider euthanasia. Your vet will be able to advise you, but the decision is ultimately yours.

Although you will be desperately upset at saying goodbye to your dearly-loved companion, remember that you are responsible for his wellbeing, and that it is your duty not to let your best friend suffer.

4 *Grooming*

Grooming is very important for an Old English Sheepdog throughout his life. You must start training your puppy for this experience very soon after you bring him home. If you have bought your puppy from a good breeder, then he will already have been taught the first steps about being groomed.

PUPPY GROOMING

You must be very firm but also kind. Never let your puppy take over and always insist that you are in control. The puppy will, perhaps, struggle and fight at first, but do not give in. Only stop grooming when you feel you are happy and that it is your choice to stop and not the puppy's decision. However, do not make the grooming sessions too lengthy.

If you are firm and keep training your puppy in the way you want to groom, you will find that he will learn to love it. When you have completed your grooming, make sure you reward him with a nice treat.

TOOLS, TABLES AND FLOOR

At first, just use a steel comb. Always groom the body first. When you have gained your puppy's confidence, then you can try to make him lie down (see page 57). When you are able to groom him lying down, and he understands what you are doing, then you will be able to care for him in the manner you prefer.

You will find that most people at the shows use a grooming table, but the floor is just as good, especially when you are grooming while watching television.

LEGS FIRST

Start with the inside of one of your Bobtail's back feet; then, from the bottom part of the foot, work upwards, along the undercarriage and between the

front legs, and then down the front leg. You now can repeat the procedure on the top part of your puppy and also along the neck and shoulders.

When you have completed this process, tell your puppy that you are going to turn him over. He will soon understand what you are doing and will lie down and await your instructions. Hold all his feet together and then roll him over on to his other side. You are now ready to repeat the process.

UPPER BODY
Having groomed both sides, and all the legs and feet, you then deal with the top part of the body. Stand your puppy and brush him from the back of the neck, down the shoulders, along the back, towards the rear end.

Then, all that remains is to groom the front under his chin and downwards. It is a good idea to let your puppy sit when you are grooming under his chin. Now you only have the head to do.

You should feel quite proud of yourself. I always start by grooming all the body first and grooming the head last, but you can do it the other way round. It does not really make any difference where you start, just as

Your puppy should be rewarded with a treat or toy at the end of every grooming session

long as you complete the whole grooming cycle.

EARS
Ears can be a big problem, on a puppy or an adult dog, if you are not careful in looking after them (page 44), so it is important that puppies are trained to allow their ears to be touched. To start with, merely play with the ears; your puppy will love a tickle just under them.

ADULT GROOMING
Adult dogs who have been properly trained love to be groomed, and really like the attention. I find the process very

Before grooming: Your Bobtail may be as loveable as ever, but he is certainly in need of a makeover!

relaxing and, of course, it really is very satisfying to see a well-groomed Bobtail.

FEET

You need to keep a check on the feet. The hair will grow between the toes and can get knotted, so you need to keep it clipped. For this job, you need a curved pair of scissors. Use them with the pointed parts of the scissors facing upwards. This way you are less likely to cut any part of the foot.

The claws will need to be clipped from time to time. Not all puppies have their dewclaws removed and they will need checking every time you are grooming. I have known them to grow and curl right round back into the dog's leg. Because dogs do not use dewclaws for anything, they really grow very quickly. You must be careful not to clip any of the claws too close to the quick or you will make the claws bleed.

Hair grows between the pads
and gets matted and tangled.

Use curved scissors to trim back the hair.

The foot after trimming.

The nails will need trimming on a
regular basis.

Use nail-clippers, and make sure you
trim the nail tip only.

EAR FLAPS

To groom the ear flaps, you need to use a stainless steel fine comb. Hairs will start to grow inside the ear flap. The vet might tell you to take these hairs out. After years of experience, I advise you not to pluck them out, but to groom them with the fine comb. You must, of course, be gentle, and not interfere with the workings of the ear in any way. If you groom the ears regularly, you will keep the deeper hairs free from matting.

OUTER EAR

The ears can get very matted if you are not careful. You need a fine stainless steel comb to groom around the edges of the ear where a thick undercoat grows. You will have to look out for this, because you can soon think that this is how hair should be on the ears of your dog. You must always be able to feel and see the edges of your pet's ears. If the ears do get very matted, this is a difficult and tedious area to groom and you can quite easily make the ear bleed. I advise you to keep a close eye on the edges of the ears and keep them knot-free.

Where the ear folds over from the top part of the head is another place that can get matted. You must always be able to lift the ears away from the side of the head and right over on to the top of the head and be able to comb the hair in layers in any direction.

Remember to take as little of the undercoat out as possible if you are going to show your dog. The head is one part of the body where you need to keep in as much undercoat as possible. If you take all the undercoat out, you will make your OES look out of balance.

When your dog is free from any knots, you only need to use your brush. One of the secrets of grooming is taking the coat in layers. You will find, when you have not groomed your dog for a short time, the hair will form ringlets, so it is quite easy to separate it into layers in any direction that suits you.

If your Bobtail has any problems or infection in the ears you must take him to the vet.

EYES

The deposit, known as sleep, which will form in the eyes, needs to be cleaned every day. Your dog will grow long eyelashes, in order to cope with the characteristic fall of facial hair.

EAR FLAPS

1. The inside ear before grooming.

2. A fine comb can be used, very gently, to keep the hair tangle-free.

3. The inside ear after grooming.

OUTER EAR

1. The hair on the outer ear tangles easily.

2. Comb the hair through in layers to get rid of mats and tangles.

TYING A TOPKNOT

Many Bobtail owners keep the hair on the head tied back to give the dog unobscured vision. But this should not be done in the run-up to a show as it spoils the natural fall of the hair

The hair is gathered up.

A band is used to secure the hair.

The topknot is folded neatly on top of the head.

FACIAL HAIR

People will ask you why you do not cut the hair from above the dog's eyes. Can he see with all that hair over his eyes? That hair is known as the fall.

The answer is that he will have no problem with it either being left just the way it grows, or if you clip it or tie it up in a topknot. There are no rules about whether an OES should have a fall or not, and it does not affect his eyesight.

Bobtails, you will find, bump into things from time to time, not because they are not able to see, but because, when they have hair over their eyes, their long eyelashes lift the hair away from their eyes, so they look downwards at the floor. I can assure you that they will bump into many things, like doors and chairs, but never seem to come to any harm.

If you are going to show your dog, I recommend that you keep the dog's hair over his eyes every day. The reason is that, if your dog has a very thick and dense head coat and you clip it, or tie it back all the time, then, when you are showing him, you will find that he may have problems seeing where

COAT CARE

1. Use a comb to groom the neck and shoulders.

4. Pay special attention to the underarms.

2. If your Bobtail lies on his side on a grooming table, it will be easier to tackle the undercarriage.

5. Move round to the front of the leg.

3. Brush through the coat, layer by layer.

6. The hair on the feet may need to be trimmed.

Front view of an OES ready for showing.

he is going and lose his confidence. I have known a dog refuse to move and just dig his feet into the ground. However, if he is used to having a natural fall of hair, then there will be no problem. You are allowed to brush the fall back when you are moving your dog in the show ring, but you will find it will automatically fall forward.

NECK AND SHOULDERS

The neck, and over the shoulders, is where you can remove most of the undercoat. Groom from the back of the neck down past the withers – from the ear to where the elbow starts, round the front from under the chin or beard. Groom down the front once again to where the elbows begin. Do this on both sides.

The hair on the rump is brushed to emphasise the rise in the dog's back.

The remaining parts of the body and legs need to be kept well coated with as much undercoat and topcoat as possible. Allow the topcoat, or guard coat, to grow quite long. As your dog grows more coat, you will have to shorten the length, mainly along the top line, over the rump. This can be done by holding the full length of the coat and, just by using scissors, cutting back to where the really loose, sparse hairs begin. You use the scissors as you would use a comb, to back-comb. Remember, your dog must not look as though you have cut the coat, and consequently have a 'blunt' finish – he must look natural. This also applies to the grooming of the feet.

CLEAN TAIL

It is very important to look after the dog's rear end. When the coat starts to grow, the dog's faeces may stick to the hair. When this happens it is not a pleasant job to clear. The best way is to soak the area with lukewarm, soapy water and, with the steel comb, just keep easing the motion away. Dry off and apply some talc.

This problem can be prevented if you trim the hair away from where the tail has been docked

An exhibitor should complement the dog, so choose a colour that will show off the Bobtail to full advantage.

and around the anus. Then train the hair above the docked part to grow so that it falls over the docked tail and the rectum because, if you intend to show the dog, it must not be obvious that you have cut any of his hair.

SHOW FINISH

When groomed, the OES should resemble a shire horse, carrying a nice, arched neck and a straight front, with a gentle rise over the loin standing four-square. The rump should be very profuse in coat. You should put your left

hand to where the gentle rise starts, holding your hand on your dog's back, then brushing his coat towards your hand, away from the stump. This will emphasise the rise on your dog's back and it is the correct way to groom.

Train your dog to stand and stay while you are grooming for the ring. Stand your dog four-square with the lead round his neck. Place the lead under the beard and at the back of the ears, just keeping it taut. Brush the hair down from the neck, past the withers, straight down from under the chin towards the elbows.

You can train your dog to allow you to lift one leg at a time. Lift a front leg, then brush from the feet towards the elbow and all around the leg. With one hand holding the leg, give a gentle shake. Then allow your dog to stand. Repeat.

Your dog will also allow you to lift the back leg. Stretch the back leg out backwards, groom all round, once again from the toes along the stifle.

Brush the coat outwards, all round the hock and up towards the rump, until you are at the centre of the rump. Repeat. Brush the coat down from the withers and from the side of the neck towards the rib cage and gently lift the coat from the undercarriage. You do not want your dog to look flat-ribbed.

Finally, brush the head by lifting the coat from under the centre of the chin outwards, up the ears, to the centre of the head at both sides. When you view your dog, look from the rear to the head and your dog should look pear-shaped. This means he has a nice, rounded rear, going gradually smaller towards the head. The head must not look too small, but be in proportion.

Then stand back and look at your artistic work.

PET TRIM

Some owners prefer their Bobtails to have a pet trim, where the coat is clipped short all over. This is usually done twice a year, around spring and autumn.

Not only does it mean less grooming for the owner, but the dogs can benefit too. Older dogs, particularly, become less patient during long grooming sessions, and enjoy the freedom that comes with their new haircut. In the

A pet trim is a sensible option for Bobtail owners who do not have the time to commit to grooming.

summer, the dogs are less hot and bothered, and in the winter it is easier to clean muddy feet and bellies with their shorter coats.

Bobtails look completely different in a pet trim, so be prepared for a shock when you first see your clipped dog!

5 Training Targets

Essentially a working dog at heart, the Bobtail is a very intelligent animal, who takes well to training. He enjoys the mental stimulation, and spending time with his owner. The key trait in a Bobtail's personality is his desire to please his owner, so he is an enthusiastic breed to work with.

Always give him lots of praise when he has done something right. You may have to give him instructions many times before he gets the message, but your patience will pay off.

You will find that the best way of making your puppy understand your commands is to use a deeper tone of voice, combined with very clear speech. He will soon recognise your 'training tone' and will realise that he is expected to work.

TRAINING CLASSES

Sign up for a training class as soon as your Bobtail is old enough (and once he has had his vaccinations), first ensuring that the training methods are reward-based, with no punishment used at all.

Training classes help puppies to socialise with other dogs. You must always be aware of these

A well-trained Bobtail will always be a pleasure to own.

Your dog must learn to walk alongside you – neither pulling ahead nor dragging behind.

other dogs. Sometimes they may seem to be friendly but will then snap at your dog for no reason whatsoever. This can really upset a youngster. In most cases, these dogs are only protecting their owner's small area, which belongs to them while they are training. It is important always to remember that dogs have their own instinctive reactions to the situations in which they find themselves.

Always take with you a dry towel and something that you can use to clear up any mess that your

puppy may make. You should, at all times, clean up anything that your dog has deposited, even when you are just taking your puppy for a walk. Always have a plastic bag of some description with you.

GETTING USED TO A LEAD

I never use collars on my dogs. Instead, I use leads that have a collar and lead all in one. You can purchase slip leads in rolled leather, which are very good, but quite expensive. The reason for not using a collar is that, if you leave one on an OES, the hair will not grow. If you do have a collar on your dog all of the time, you must keep it fairly loose, so that the coat will not be affected. You must remember, when you take your puppy out, to fasten the collar tight enough so that it will not slip over his head.

Once you have started training, and your puppy understands the procedure, you can start putting a loose lead around his neck. You will be able to do this while you are relaxing, reading or watching TV, or when your puppy is playing with toys. You will find that he will just ignore the lead or will start to chew and play with it, thinking that it is a new toy.

Command your dog to "Stay".

Leave your dog, and as you turn and face him, repeat the command "Stay".

Give the command "Come", sounding bright and welcoming, and you should be rewarded with an enthusiastic response.

When you think your puppy is not bothered about the lead, you can start holding it. You may find that he will pull and cry and try to get away from you. The object is not to let him pull; you must try to keep a loose lead at all times. If you pull, the puppy will pull automatically against you; it is the natural thing to do, especially if he thinks that he will be able to get free.

LEAD-WALKING

When your puppy settles down, you can take him into your garden to practise walking on the lead. Try to walk him in a triangle. If possible, move together, with your puppy on your left-hand side. Hold the loop of the lead in your right hand, with the left hand holding the lead nearer to the dog's neck. By doing this, you will have more control.

Speak to your puppy at all times, and give instructions about the direction in which you intend to move. Walk on and then move in a triangle; the puppy will soon start to listen and await your instructions. If he starts to walk in front of you, say "Heel". If he takes no notice of you, then you must turn to the right, so that he then finds himself behind you.

You may have to repeat this action for some time before your puppy realises that he is always going to be behind. Eventually, he will get used to the idea of heeling.

Once you have mastered the art of 'doing a triangle' nicely and steadily together, then you will be able to move your puppy in any direction with ease. You need to be able to move in a triangle and also straight up and down. These are the ways in which you will be requested to move when in a show ring.

COMING WHEN CALLED

As soon as your puppy enters your home, you must use his name, so that he gets accustomed to it. Then add the instruction "Come". Do make sure that he responds to this instruction, no matter which member of the family issues it.

Puppies love being with people, so this exercise is quite simple. As your Bobtail gets older, however, he may be more reluctant to come when called, preferring to be elsewhere instead. If your Bobtail doesn't come, make yourself more appealing. Call him in a more excited tone of voice, wave your hands, or run in the opposite direction. He will be puzzled by this behaviour, and will soon run

to you to see what's going on! Keep treats in your pocket, and give them to him randomly when he comes to you, as a reward for his obedience – he'll be more likely to return to you if he thinks there will be something in it for him.

SIT

The Sit is one of the most important commands. With it, you can control your dog in a number of situations and can immediately stop whatever he is doing!

The Sit is an easy exercise to teach – especially when a treat is on offer!

THE DOWN

Start with your dog in the Sit, and encourage him to go into the Down with a treat (above).

When your dog is in the Down, make sure he stays in position for a few moments before allowing him to move (right).

- Hold a tidbit in one hand, positioned in front of your dog's nose.
- As he looks up at the treat, move it up and towards your dog so that it is an inch (2.5 cms) or so above his head.
- As he looks up to get the treat, his bottom will go down. As soon as it touches the floor, say "Sit" and give him the treat – and lots of praise.

As with all aspects of training, practise little and often until it becomes second nature to your Bobtail, and eventually he will sit on the verbal command alone.

DOWN
- Ask your puppy to "Sit" (see above).
- Now show your puppy a treat in your hand again, and move your hand downwards to the floor, a short distance in front of the puppy. Do this slowly, allowing your puppy to follow your hand and the treat with his nose.
- Your Bobtail will have to lie on the floor in order to reach the treat. It may take him a while to work this out, but he'll get there in the end.
- As soon as he does lie down, say

"Down", give him the treat, and praise him.

- Keep practising, and he will get quicker, and will soon go Down when asked, without having to be lured with a treat.

WAIT

Train your puppy to Wait. You will find this immensely useful in a number of situations. For example, when letting your Bobtail out of the car, you can instruct him to Wait while you put his lead on and take control of him, rather than have him racing out, possibly on to a busy road. Other situations include:

- When you want to wipe his feet when you have been out for a walk
- When you have bathed your puppy and want to dry him and rub him down with a towel
- When going through a door, you can tell your dog to wait while you go ahead first.

The Wait command can be a difficult one, as Bobtail puppies love being active. Do not attempt this command until your puppy will sit on command.

- Stand opposite the puppy and ask him to "Sit".
- Step forward, remove his lead,

Start with your dog in the Sit and command him to "Stay", backing up the verbal command with a hand signal.

Build up the Stay in easy stages, gradually extending the distance you leave your dog.

The Down Stay is a useful exercise to teach, and many dogs feel more secure when left in this position.

The Wait command is used in a variety of different situations.

and say "Stay" firmly. When giving the command, hold your hand up, with your palm facing your dog.

- Take one step back, still keeping your hand raised and still maintaining eye contact with your pup.
- Then step forward, praise him, and give him a treat as a reward.
- Over several practice sessions, take more steps away from your dog until he will reliably Wait from you at a distance.

If your puppy breaks the Stay, don't be cross – that will make him insecure, and even more unlikely to Wait. Instead, simply return to him, ask him to sit, and start the exercise again.

THE RETRIEVE

Once your Bobtail has learnt the

The OES can be trained to retrieve. This provides good exercise, as well as interaction between dog and owner.

basic exercises (above), there is no end to what you can go on to teach him. One fun exercise is the retrieve – which also comes in very useful when you want your dog to fetch the newspaper in the morning!

- Throw a soft toy or ball for your Bobtail, and ask him to "Fetch". Even young puppies will chase after the toy, and will usually mouth the toy.
- When he has the toy in his mouth, call him to you straight away. Be really excited so he comes to you – hopefully, with the toy still in his mouth. If he doesn't come with the toy, keep practising, and move closer to the dog so he doesn't have very far to come.

- When he comes to you with the toy in his mouth, give him lots of praise, and throw the item immediately for him to play with again.
- When he knows what is expected of him, you can progress to other objects, such as the newspaper, or his own lead.

THE STAND

You must train your puppy to 'stand'. It is a must in show dogs, but is also important for when you groom your OES, or take him to the vet's.

To hold your puppy in a standing position, place one hand under his chin and the other hand under his hind legs. You may do

With practice, your Bobtail will learn to stand in a show pose.

Showing is an absorbing hobby, and it can be very competitive at the top level.

Last-minute preparations before the dog goes into the ring.

Your dog must be trained to stand in show pose for a judge's assessment.

Each dog will be given an individual examination.

The judge will look at movement, which, to the expert eye, can reveal a lot about the dog's conformation.

this on a table. This will also help your puppy to get used to being stood on a table. Do this procedure as often as possible and certainly every time you groom him. You will find that the puppy will soon get used to standing. You must train him to stand for a few minutes longer each time, until you find that you have to tell him when he can move. It will take quite a long time before he will stand on his own without you having to hold him.

OBEDIENCE AND AGILITY

Apart from the show ring, there are other events in which you can participate with your Bobtail. Several OES have been trained for Agility and Obedience competitions.

Agility involves taking your dog over a series of obstacles, quickly and accurately. It is a fun sport, which most dogs love, and is a good way of exercising your dog's mind and body. It is very popular, and there are hundreds of clubs which teach the sport, and lots of opportunities to compete at different levels. Your national kennel club will have details of your nearest Agility training club.

Obedience is another option, which involves various exercises to test your dog's Obedience ability and your control of the dog. The exercises get progressively more difficult according to the level at which you compete. Again, it is a popular pastime, and there are many clubs which specialise in competitive Obedience. Ask your kennel club for details.

SHOW TRAINING

When you first take your dog to a show-training class you will find people are very helpful and will show you the correct procedure. Your dog will also get used to being handled and inspected by strangers.

Once you have achieved all of the set procedures, then is the time to take your puppy to the sort of show that you think you are able to handle. The trainers at the class will give you advice on how to start your show career.

THERAPY DOGS

Once you have a well-trained, well-socialised dog, you might also like to consider offering your services to therapy dog work. This involves taking your dog to various establishments where people do not have access to pets (such as hospitals, residential homes etc.). Interacting with animals has been shown to have lots of benefits – improving people's moods, and also, in some cases, their health. It also gives people the opportunity to chat with the dog's owner, too.

Several organisations arrange these visiting schemes, and your national kennel club should be able to give you their details.

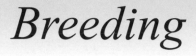

6 *Breeding*

If you are thinking of breeding a litter of puppies, seriously consider the work involved and the experience required. Bringing eight or so little lives into the world is a big responsibility, and that responsibility stays with the breeder for the entire length of the puppies' lives. If you use less than perfect parents, you will not only be jeopardising the puppies' well-being, but you could harm the future of the breed, so breeding is a job best left to the experts.

Certainly do not be tempted to breed puppies, thinking it is an easy way to get rich – it is not! Once you have paid all the vet fees, extra heating and feeding costs etc., you will be lucky to have any money left.

BREEDING PLAN

The time to start thinking of having a litter should be when your bitch is about three years old. You must be sure that she has the correct qualities and that you are ready to take this step. It is very important that you breed only from good specimens, because you should be breeding for the future of our wonderful Old English Sheepdogs.

You need to choose a good, sound, upstanding male who does not have any outstanding faults. Look for a dog with plenty of bone and substance, with a profuse coat, good both in texture and colour, with no hint of brown or sable. He must be able to cover the ground with ease and move with you freely in all directions. He needs to have a very good temperament and a lovely nature.

Ask the owners of various stud dogs for a copy of their dog's pedigree. Ask an experienced breeder to help you analyse the dog's ancestors to ascertain whether the dogs are related in some way and to find a suitable partner that will complement your

The aim of every breeder is to produce sound, healthy animals that are typical of the breed. This is a group of Champions bred by the author.

own dog's characteristics. Do not just use the dog down the lane, because he lives close by.

Make sure that both your bitch and the stud dog have been X-rayed for hip dysplasia and that the scores are good.

ORGANISING A MATING

When a bitch is going to be mated, do not feed either the dog or the bitch, as the excitement can make them sick. Decide on the place where you wish the mating to take place. Allow the dog and bitch to meet each other, keeping the bitch on the lead. Allow the dog plenty of time.

When he is ready to mate, the owner of the bitch should hold her head very firmly and make sure it is away from the dog, because some bitches can be very aggressive.

Sometimes you may need to raise the floor for the dog if the bitch is on the large size. I always put an old rug down, which prevents the dogs from slipping and provides a little bit of comfort for you.

THE TIE

When the dog ties with the bitch,

he will usually let all his weight go on to her and completely relax. After a few moments, he will then try to lift one of his legs over her. This is part of the normal process but it is best not to allow your dog to turn too soon. Hold your arms completely around both the dog and bitch. After a few moments, you will be able to allow your dog to turn. The dog and bitch will then be back to back.

They can be tied for varying lengths of time, from as little as four minutes up to an hour or more. I once had a dog and bitch whose mating lasted for well over an hour.

POST-MATING

When the mating is over, keep the bitch quiet for as long as possible. She should have a drink if she wants one. The stud dog should

Pedigrees must be researched thoroughly before planning a mating.

Treat your bitch as naturally as possible in the first weeks of her pregnancy.

be taken away from the bitch as soon as possible after the mating. Make sure that he is back to normal. Cleanse him with an antiseptic wipe, just in case of any infection.

THE PREGNANT BITCH

Let your bitch behave as normal. You will find, however, that she may completely change in her whole attitude. Some bitches, like humans, have morning sickness or, at about three weeks, have a stomach upset. She will not want

anything to eat and may be very miserable. Just try to feed her the things you know that she likes.

If you are not sure, about four weeks after the mating, whether the bitch is in whelp or not, you can arrange to have her scanned. If she has a clear, sticky discharge coming from the vagina, this is usually a good sign that she is in whelp.

From six weeks onwards, when the puppies start to grow, you must start to feed your bitch good nursing food, including fresh meat, fish, eggs, milk and puddings; anything that you know she likes, plus vitamins and calcium. Do not give any kind of fatty foods. They just upset the stomach. Always make sure she has plenty of fresh water available to drink.

If your bitch is able to take milk every day, this a good form of calcium which benefits her and helps in the growth of the puppies.

THE WHELPING AREA

Build your whelping box in a nice, quiet, peaceful place. Your bitch will want to be kept away from any interruptions. The size should be at least 6 feet x 4 feet (1.83 m x 1.22 m), with two full sides, and the remaining two sides split into two parts, a third and a two-thirds, so that you are able to build the sides up as the puppies get more active.

You also need to put pieces of dowelling or wood across all the insides of the box. If a puppy creeps behind the mother, the wood will stop the mother from lying on the puppy. My advice is that you do not leave the mother and puppies alone until the puppies are at least two weeks old or have their eyes open. This

means at night as well as in the daytime. You need to organise family shifts. This will help everyone to become involved.

You need some kind of heating for the new-born pups. An infrared lamp is best if you live in a cold climate. This needs to hang above the whelping box so that the bitch will not knock it when she is getting in and out of this area. Keep the puppies away from any draughts.

VETERINARY ADVICE

If, at any stage of the process, you have any concerns about your dog or puppies' health, seek veterinary advice immediately.

LABOUR SIGNS

From about the 54th day onwards, start taking the bitch's temperature. It should drop from 38 degrees to 37 degrees Centigrade (100.4 to 98.6 degrees F) or even less. Check the temperature last thing at night. You will find that it is higher in the evening than in the morning. If the temperature starts to increase, and stays high, you must contact your vet as you may have a problem.

The litter pictured at two days old.

Usually, you know when your bitch is going to start to whelp. When everyone has gone to bed in the household, your bitch will relax, but if the pups are imminent, she will not let you settle. She will keep making beds in different places and scratching in corners.

BIRTH OF A LITTER
It is wonderful to see a puppy being born, in its water sac with the placenta still attached to the brood bitch. Sometimes, the bitch can be very rough and cause a lot of bleeding when breaking the umbilical cord. If you need to intervene, then cut the cord with a pair of sterilized scissors, about an inch from the puppy's stomach.

Examine each puppy for any hernia that may have been caused when being born and seek veterinary advice if you have any concerns.

When your bitch has had her first puppy, she will wash him,

sometimes until the puppy is completely wet through. This is why it is so important to have the room nicely warmed, without being overheated.

When your bitch is ready to have another puppy, she will put her head down and stretch her neck right out. This is the sign of another contraction. Some bitches will sit up when they are having further contractions and you can feel the puppy move along the womb.

While your bitch is having further puppies, put those that have already been born into a separate box or basket to keep them nice and warm. Put a sheet of newspaper over them, which helps retain the heat.

As each puppy is born, you must let the bitch look after him or her. Once she has cleaned the puppy, then make sure he can start to feed naturally. It is very important that each puppy takes its first milk from the bitch; this is very rich in vitamins and protective antibodies for a newly-born puppy.

When each puppy is born, keep a record of its sex, weight and markings. If your bitch has a large

It does not take long before the puppies are quite happy to eat solid food.

Development is incredibly rapid in the first few weeks. These puppies are six weeks old.

litter, it is not always easy to remember which puppy was born first. If you keep a record of each puppy's weight, you will soon know if all the puppies are healthy and growing.

REARING THE PUPS

Make sure the puppies stay clean and warm, and mum will do the rest. Change the bedding in the whelping box regularly, and check the temperature in the room. Even in summer months, the night temperature may be cold enough to warrant extra heating. In such instances, an overhead heat lamp (placed at just above the height of an adult Bobtail standing up) will be necessary.

Around two weeks of age, when the puppies open their eyes, you can start weaning them. Start by giving them a little evaporated milk, and progress on to more solid foods, such as rice puddings, and then mashed meat.

Gradually increase the amount of food you give to the puppies, working up to more and more solid foods, and they will start to take less from the mother as they grow.

EXTRA ADVICE

If you have any queries, or need advice about breeding, whelping and rearing, your own dog's breeder (or your vet) should be able to help.

7 *Health Care*

T his chapter tells you about some health problems which your Old English Sheepdog might develop. However, it is always best, if you think your dog is looking a bit off-colour, to consult your vet.

PROTECTION

You must have your dog vaccinated against a number of diseases. These vary from country to country, but generally include distemper, hepatitis, leptospirosis, parvovirus, and parainfluenza. You should ask your breeder about what vaccinations have been given before you collect your puppy. As soon as you have brought your puppy home, you must make an appointment with your vet to have him checked over and the vaccination programme completed.

Remember that the puppy should be protected from likely

The OES is generally a healthy breed.

sources of infection until the vaccination programme is complete, but this should not interfere with his early socialisation programme.

It is important that you do not let your dog's immunity decline. Do make sure that he gets his annual boosters.

A-Z OF COMMON AILMENTS

ARTHRITIS

Arthritis is very common in dogs; mainly older dogs are affected. There are lots of different treatments available, including homoeopathic ones.

To find the best treatment that will help your dog, take the advice of your vet.

CANKER

Canker is a problem with the ears, but if you follow my grooming instructions for the ears (see Chapter 4), hopefully this problem will not arise.

Canker is caused by ear mites. The symptoms include dark brown wax building up inside the ear. Your dog will keep scratching and shaking his head and holding it to one side. The ears can get very inflamed and sore, and veterinary advice is then required.

DEAFNESS

Deafness seems to be associated with colour. Dogs which are predominantly white, with blue eyes and no pigmentation, appear to suffer more than dogs with dark markings and plenty of pigmentation.

If a dog is totally deaf, he can be very difficult to train, although it is possible to achieve this through hand signals. A deaf dog must never be let free at any time, because he will have no sense of danger and, unless you and the dog have eye contact, the dog would not hear the sounds of danger and could be involved in an accident, especially on the road. He will need a great deal of attention at all times and will never react as quickly as totally sound animals.

DIARRHOEA

Feeding cooked meat to your dog can upset his stomach quite easily. The fat content will cause the dog to have loose motions. If you do cook the meat, always make sure that you skim off most of the fat when the meat has cooled down. You will need to starve the dog for 24 hours, letting him have only small amounts of glucose and water, just a few drops at a time.

The glucose will help to restore energy.

Sometimes when dogs are sick they will keep drinking. This is why you should restrict him to having small amounts until you are sure he can take a normal drink. However, it is important that you give him enough water so that he does not dehydrate.

After 24 hours, you need to start feeding him, but only with white meats such as chicken and fish, or cheese, yogurt and boiled rice. You must make sure the chicken and fish are fresh and throughly cooked, and cold when given to the dog. If in any doubt, consult your vet.

ECLAMPSIA

This is when the bitch has put all her energy into labour contract-ions causing her to drain her system of calcium. You must act very quickly and get the vet, who will give her a calcium injection. This injection will usually be given directly into the vein. You will find your bitch will respond within only a few minutes.

Give your bitch drinks of egg beaten into milk and plenty of glucose. This will help give her a little more strength during her whelping.

Puppies must not be allowed outside the garden until they have completed their vaccination course.

ECZEMA

Eczema can be a recurring complaint and you must seek veterinary advice to try to keep the condition under control. There are two kinds: wet eczema and dry eczema. Both cause very red and inflamed skin.

Eczema is caused by a number of different things, including hormone imbalances and food allergies. A diet that is too high in protein or lacking in oil and fat can create problems, as can parasites such as mites under the skin, and fleas, if the coat is not kept in good, clean condition. That is why you must keep your dog well groomed, which keeps the coat clean.

Grass seeds can also cause skin disorders. They can penetrate under the skin and cause irritation. Always check the pads and toes when you have been exercising your dog in grass, especially in the summertime.

EYE PROBLEMS

There are a number of problems which affect eyes. The most common ones are entropion and progressive retinal atrophy, both of which are hereditary.

Entropion is the condition where the eyelid curls back into the eye. This causes the eyelash to keep rubbing against the eyeball and makes the eye really sore, causing tears to keep forming. The condition may affect both eyes and all of the eyelids, or just one lid. An operation can be performed to rectify the problem, but such dogs could still pass the problem on to any progeny.

The operation involves making a slight slit under or over the eyelid to remove a small amount of skin, thus making it possible for

the eyelid to remain in the correct position.

Progressive retinal atrophy (PRA) is also known as night blindness. You can have your dog's eyes tested to see if this condition is present, particularly if you intend to breed from a dog or bitch.

Normally this condition develops later in life but, if your dog has a problem bumping into things when very young, look into his eyes. If the pupil stays enlarged, this could well be the sign of a problem and you should seek further advice. The condition progressively degenerates into blindness.

However, in the case of Old English Sheepdogs, do remember that they are prone to bumping into furniture, particularly when the fall of hair starts to grow over their eyes, and this does not necessarily mean that they have PRA.

FLEAS

Fleas are one of the biggest nightmares for dog owners, especially owners of multi-dog households. Inspect your dog regularly for any evidence of fleas or flea dirt, and treat him regularly with an appropriate treatment.

Your vet will be able to recommend the safest, most effective products. Spot-on treatments are particularly good, especially for long-coated breeds such as the Old English. Just part the fur over the shoulder blades and squeeze the drops on to the skin for complete protection of your dog.

As well as treating your Old English, you should also treat your home with a household flea treatment. Bedding and curtains should be cleaned regularly, and carpets should be treated and vacuumed thoroughly.

HEATSTROKE

A dog that is suffering from heatstroke will have a very high temperature, will be in great distress and may possibly pass out. You must cool his body down with a hosepipe, or even submerge the dog in cool – *not cold* – water, because this may cause more problems. Ice cubes put on the back of the neck will help.

It is not a good idea to take your dog out with you in the car if you know that the weather is going to be hot. *You must never leave your dog unattended in a car with no ventilation.* This can be fatal. A dog's temperature will rise extremely quickly in a closed car. The car will be just like a greenhouse. It will only take a few minutes for your dog to pass out. Even if you leave the window slightly open and you think you dog will be safe, *beware.* The temperature can still rise to fatal levels.

When you have got your dog's temperature under control, let him recover in a cool place and make sure he has a drink of salted water. You should use a dessertspoonful of salt to a litre of water (1.76 UK pints/2.11 US pints).

When you are travelling on a hot day with your dog in the car, you should always have a towel with you. Soak the towel in cold water and cover your dog with it. This will help keep your dog's temperature down. Remember, the car will overheat if you are stuck in a traffic jam. When you are moving you are able to keep cool by opening the windows. Take water for your dog to drink, but let him drink only small amounts at a time, not a bowlful.

HIP DYSPLASIA (HD)

HD is a very big problem in a number of breeds. Even when breeding from a dog or a bitch that are both free of HD, this does not ensure that the progeny will be completely free of it.

It is very important that all young puppies have plenty of rest and they must never be overexercised or overfed. In my experience, puppies do a lot of their own exercising every day and sleep a great deal. Puppies carrying too much weight will be prone to HD.

A dog must be at least twelve months old before being X-rayed for a hip score. The method of scoring varies under different national systems. Never breed from a dog with a bad hip score, but also do not breed just for hips. It is the whole dog which is important.

KENNEL COUGH

Ask your vet about the treatment for, and prevention of, kennel cough. This disease can make your dog quite sick and most good boarding kennels will require that you have your dog vaccinated against it if you are using their facilities. The vaccine is administered by nasal spray, not injection.

LAMENESS

If your dog shows any signs of lameness, you must seek veterinary advice as soon as possible. Your dog may not have done anything too serious, but you will need to know the correct treatment in order to deal with the injury.

PYOMETRA

Pyometra is an infection of the womb. Symptoms include: a glassy look about the eyes, lack of appetite, increased thirst, and sickness. The bitch may have a temperature, but this is not always the case. There will also be a nasty discharge from the vulva that will be dark green or red in colour.

In some cases, bitches may have a 'sealed pyometra', where there is no discharge, and so it is much more difficult to detect. If you see any of the outward signs mentioned above, do see the vet urgently, because your bitch will probably need surgery very quickly. If detected very early, the condition sometimes can be treated with strong antibiotics, although removal of the womb is the usual course of action.

WORMS

You need to worm your dog regularly against a variety of different worms, such as roundworm and tapeworm. In some countries, treatment for other types of worm, such as heartworm, is also necessary.

Medication can vary between countries.

Very young puppies can be wormed when only a few days old with a liquid mixture obtained through your vet. You are able to tell whether young puppies have worms because their stomachs will be distended. Their motions will contain very small white eggs, a bit like white spots.

Follow the instructions the vet gives you for worming your dog or puppy.

WRY MOUTH

A wry mouth is when a dog is not able to close his mouth completely. Such a dog must never be bred from. The condition occurs when the large back teeth, or molars, are too big. It is hereditary and difficult to eradicate.

You are always taking a chance when you breed from a dog with a defective mouth. An undershot mouth is when the bottom jaw closes completely over the top teeth. An overshot mouth is when the top teeth are too far over the bottom teeth. You will be able to put a finger in between the top and bottom teeth. You usually find that the dog's under-jaw will be very narrow and the mouth looks to be pointed, very much like a mouse.

SUNSTROKE

It is possible for your dog to get sunstroke. Always try to keep him in the shade, and do not let him lie in the hot sun. The symptoms of sunstroke are very much like having a stomach upset. The dog may want to drink a lot of water, and then start to be sick. He may also have diarrhoea. If you suspect your dog is suffering from sunstroke, consult a vet immediately.